Meditation is Magic:

A MAGICAL GUIDE TO PRACTICING MEDITATION AND MINDFULNESS

(Meditation is boring enough. The instruction book might as well be fun.)

Copyright © 2020 All Rights Reserved
by Rabbi Brian Zachary Mayer

All rights reserved. This book or any portion thereof may not be reproduced or used in any manner whatsoever without the express written permission of the publisher except for the use of brief quotations in a book review. And, if you are writing a review, we hope you think the book is awesome.

Printed in the United States of America

First Printing, 2020
#JFST

978-0-9800234-5-9

Religion-Outside-The-Box

ROTB.org

Dedications

Ylain G. Mayer (rB's mom, who taught him about art) • **Joe Deissroth** (Bill's high school art teacher) • **Social workers and therapists** (because they help us all get through life) • **Gordon A. Mackenzie** (who wrote *Orbiting the Giant Hairball* which inspired all who worked on this project to be unafraid to go a little bit out there) • **Our beta-readers and advice givers** (Mike S, Mary B, Allison H, Erik H, Dan R, Jason S, Bob B, Casey H., Greg R, Derrin B, Michael & Wendy R, and Carol M.) • **Moses** (Dana and Bill's dog) • And, finally, we want to acknowledge this person whose name is written here by hand: _____.

Why this label?

PARENTAL ADVISORY EXPLICIT CONTENT

Parental Advisory

We wanted kids – teens especially — to feel encouraged to tell (advise) their parents they want to learn how to meditate.

Explicit Content

ex•plic•it : /ik'splisit/

    stated clearly and in detail, leaving no room for confusion or doubt.

We set out to make these instructions about mindfulness and meditation to be explicit. Clearly stated. In detail. Leaving no room for confusion or doubt.

Also, the horse and rB both drop the f*bomb.

Rabbi Brian   *Dana*   *Bill*

Rabbi Brian (author) Dana & Bill (co-author & illustrator, married by RB in 2017)

Meditation
A magical guide to practicing meditation and mindfulness

is Magic:

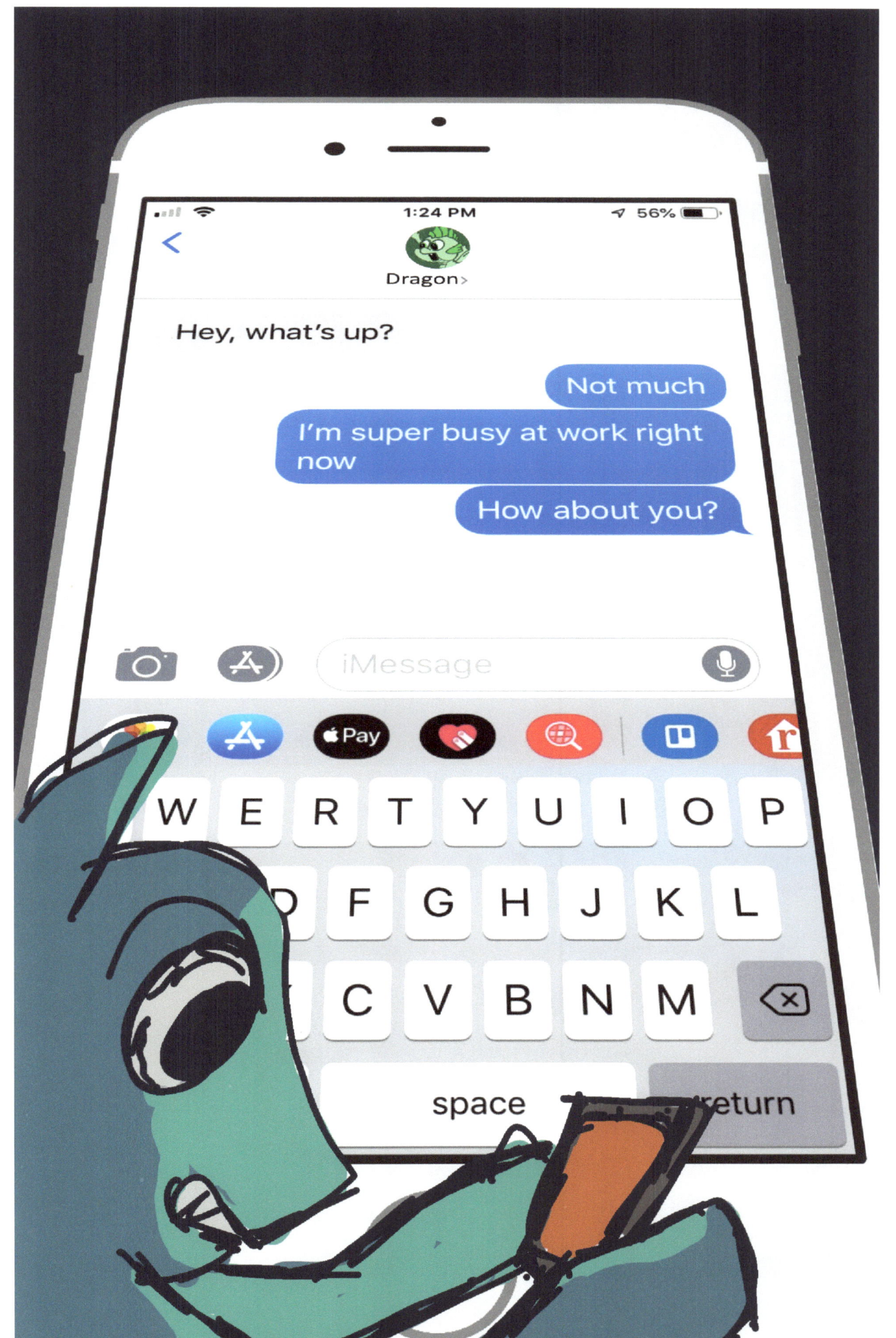

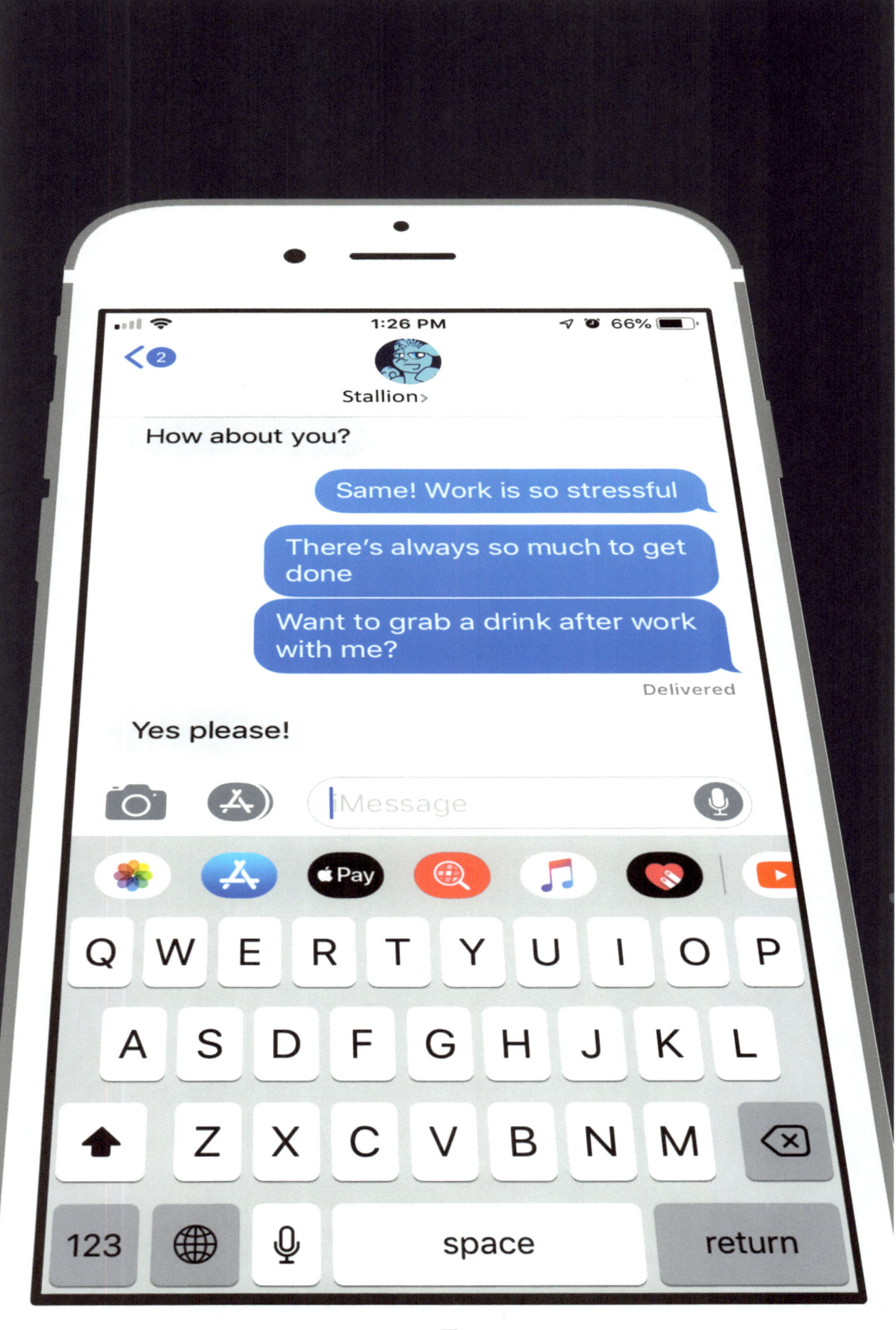

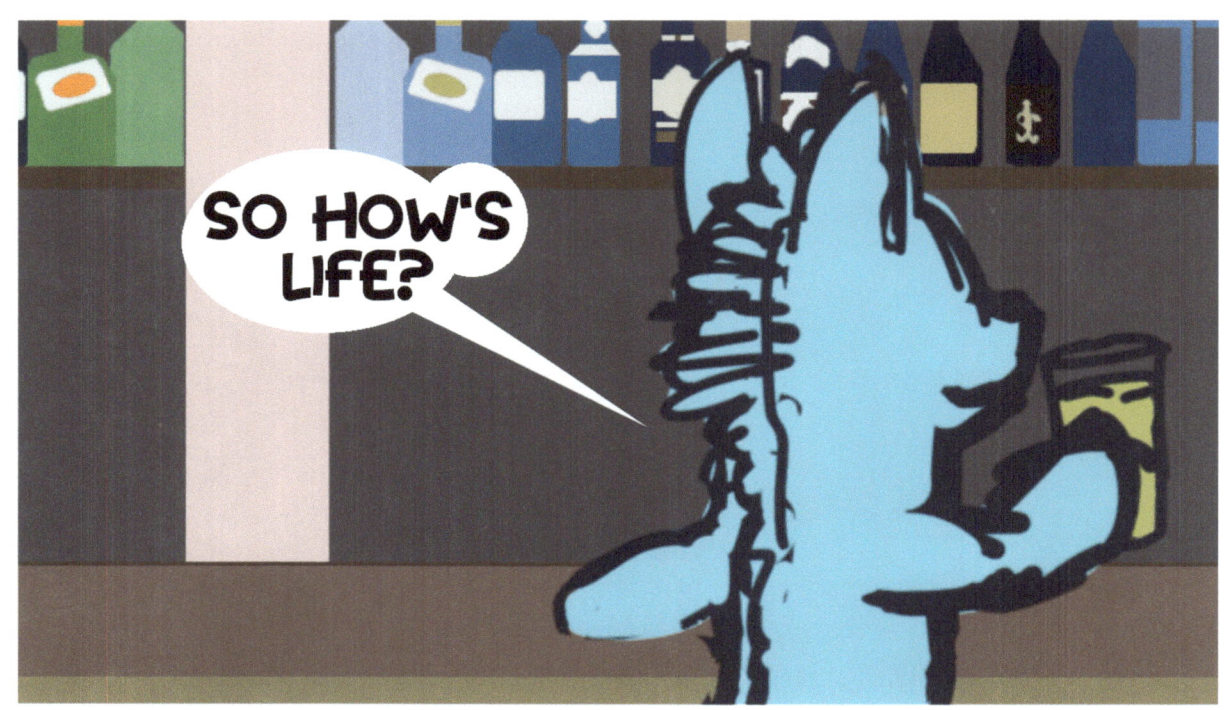

WTF!?

RABBI BRIAN!?
SAY, DON'T YOU KNOW A THING OR TWO ABOUT MEDITATION AND ALL THAT GOOD STUFF?

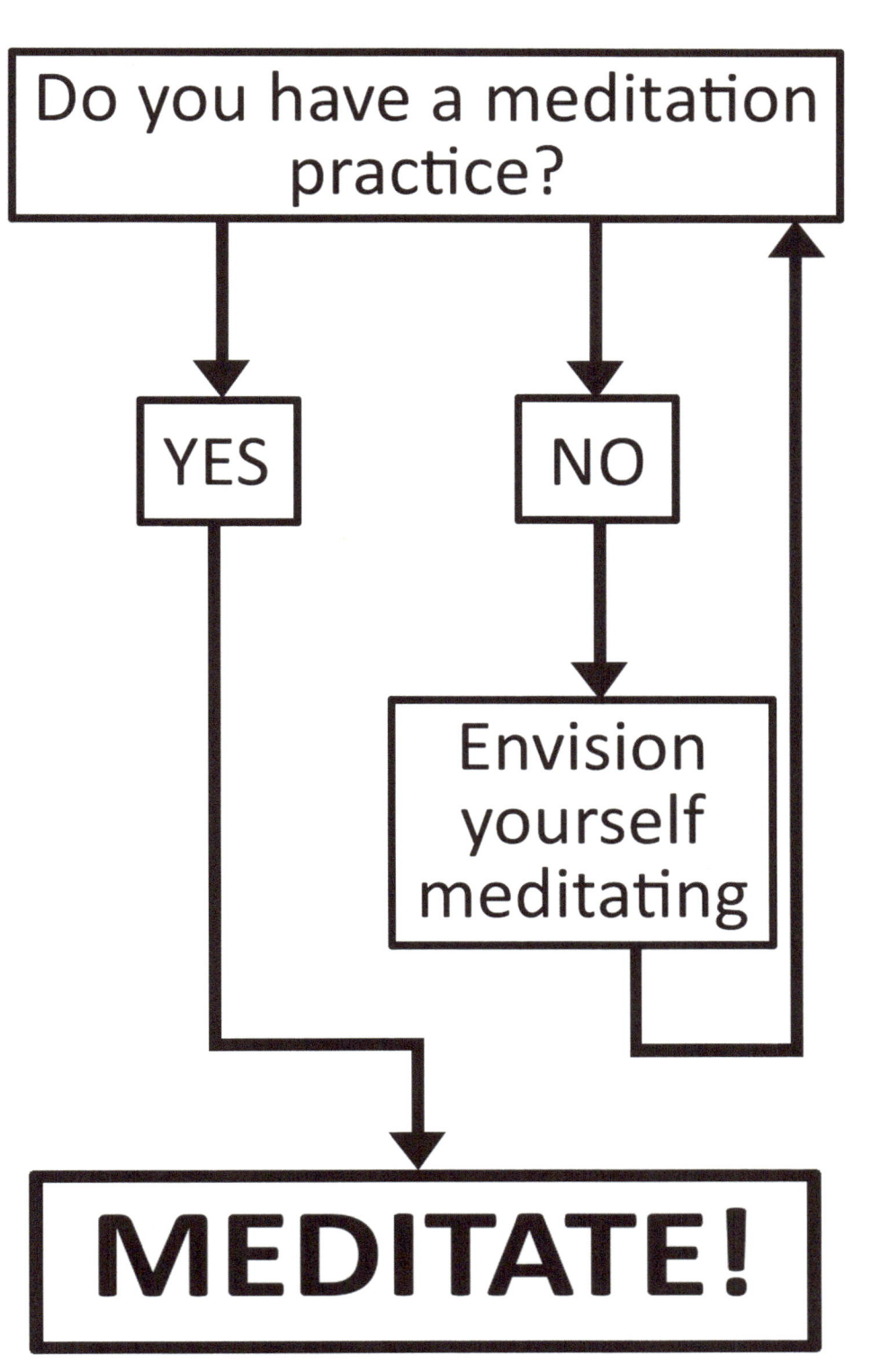

SOME SAY THEY ARE TOO BUSY.

SOME SAY THEY AREN'T COMFORTABLE SITTING STILL FOR 10 MINUTES.

WHO SAID YOU ARE SUPPOSED TO BE COMFORTABLE SITTING STILL FOR 10 MINUTES?

MOREOVER, IF YOU THINK MEDITATION WOULD HELP YOU GET COMFORTABLE SITTING STILL AND YOU WANT TO BE ABLE TO SIT STILL, IT WOULD MAKE SENSE THAT YOU WOULD THEN WANT TO MEDITATE, NOT AVOID MEDITATING.

SOME SAY THEY CAN'T QUIET THEIR MINDS.

WHO SAID YOU ARE SUPPOSED TO HAVE A QUIET MIND IN THE FIRST PLACE?

RESEARCHERS AT THE UNIVERSITY OF VIRGINIA SHOW THAT PEOPLE (I DON'T KNOW ABOUT HORSES OR DRAGONS) WOULD RATHER DO ALMOST ANYTHING RATHER THAN SIT QUIETLY.

https://rotb.org/hatemeditation/

Mindfulness

Rabbi Brian's Guide To:

MINDFULNESS

Mindfulness is really about noticing (and sitting with) what is going on in your mind. Not judging.

Sounds easy enough, right?

And it is pretty easy and gets easier with practice.

Here are the three steps toward doing mindfulness the Rabbi Brian way ...

So, you, dear reader, really, play along. Think about what you are noticing right now. (If you need a hint, you are looking at a kinda-psychedelic book about meditation and mindfulness and the rabbi character in the book just broke the fourth wall to directly address you. You've probably got some thoughts about that.) So, what are you noticing?

THINK ABOUT THE THOUGHTS YOU ARE THINKING.

2.

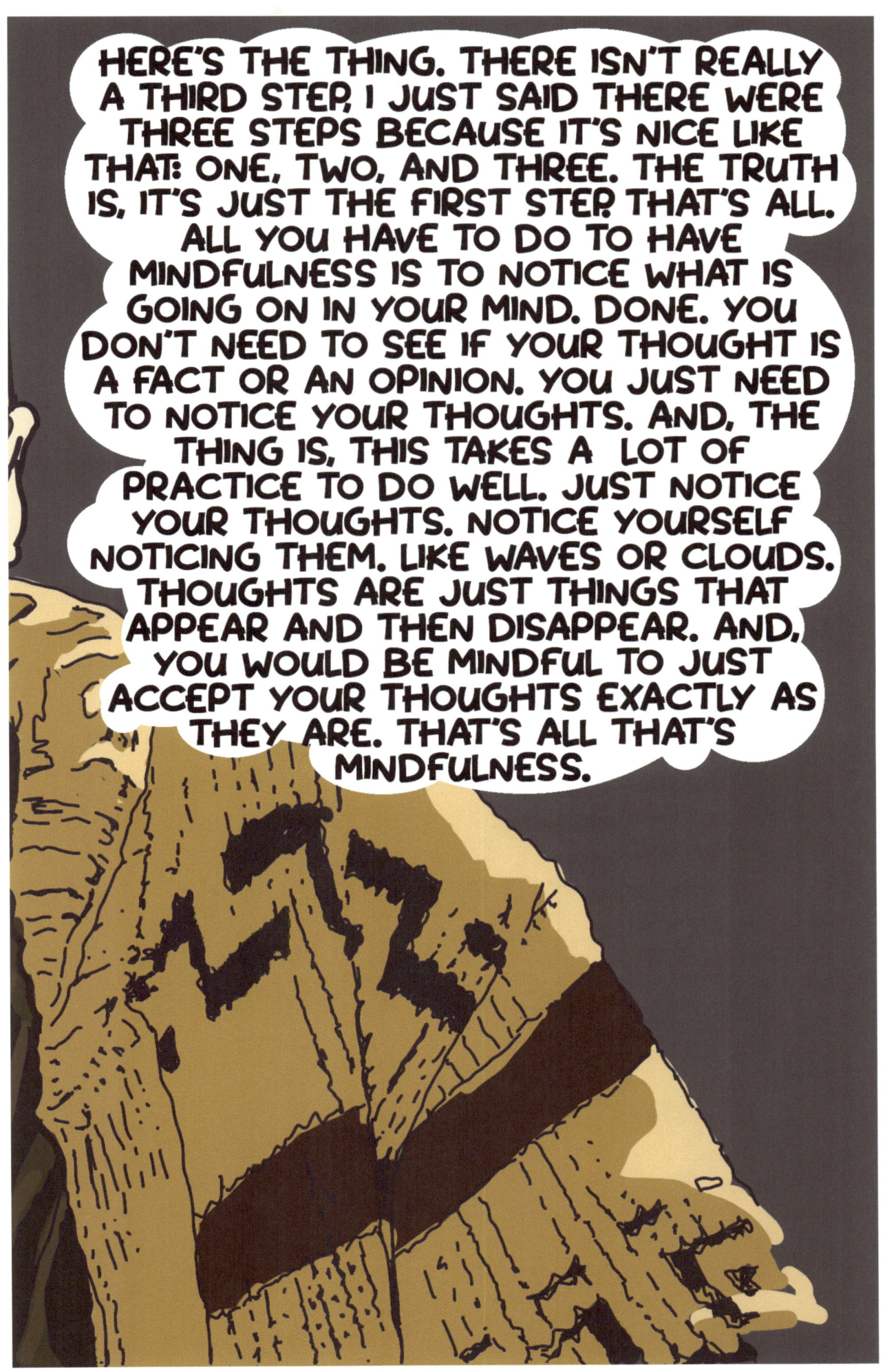

Meditation

You know everything you need to know to meditate!

Meditation is nothing more than an extended period of mindfulness. You can think of meditation as a focused period of mindfulness.

Close your eyes and do mindfulness for a few minutes and you can call yourself a meditator.

Remember:
> Notice your thoughts
> Learn to be (somewhat or a bit more) comfortable with the thoughts of your mind (without trying to steer)
> You don't have to believe every thought you have

Rabbi Brian's Guide To:

MEDITATION

Now that we've talked about mindfulness, let me cycle back and explain how meditation works.

All of meditation can be summed up in just **FOUR SIMPLE LETTERS.**

"Hey... you need more than four letters to write meditation!"

STALLION

"Yo Einstein! Let the Rabbi explain."

JOVIAL
FILLING
SUPER
TRANSFORMATION?

JUNK
FAX
STOCK
TRANSFER?

JOURNAL OF FOOD
SCIENCE AND
TECHNOLOGY?

JOINT
FIRE
SUPPORT
TEAM?

JUMPING FURRY
SALTED T-REX?

JEWISH
FEMALE
SOUL
TRANSCENDENCE?

JANE FINDS
STUPIDITY
TORTUOUS?

JOINTS FOR
SOME TURKEY?

I recommend beginners start with sitting for 15 minutes a day.

Do it for a few days in a row so you can get a sense of what it's really about.

If you can do it at the same time each day, the better.

Not in a particular posture, not with any mantra, not with any special breathing. But, to just sit – or lay down – with a timer set for 15 minutes.

Notice what you notice.

Some days I start anxious and I end anxious. Some days I start calm and end asleep and get scared by the alarm. Some days I just do my to-do list in my head. Some days it's the only peace and quiet in my whole day. Some days I really don't want to sit and some days I skip it altogether.

Just notice what you notice. Be mindful. Learn more about what's going on in your mind.

It's amazing how scary it can be
to just sit with our own thoughts.
https://rotb.org/hatemeditation/

- Four days a week, three weeks a month.
- For 20 minutes.
- Eyes closed.
- At 2pm daily laying down.
- Looking at a candle.
- Five minutes twice a day.
- Sitting on the floor.
- With a timer set.
- With or without a candle.
- J.F.S.T.
- Watching your breath. Or not.
- Love yourself.

<Option: insert bell sound>

MEDITATE NOW

FOR THE AMOUNT OF TIME OF YOUR CHOOSING.

BUT, HEY, IT'S WHAT I'M DOING AND IT'S NOT SO BAD.

I JUST DON'T LIKE IT. AND, THAT'S OK.

I DON'T LIKE DRY HAY MUCH EITHER. ALTHOUGH, I AM HUNGRY... I MIGHT WANT TO GET SOME HAY LATER.

... JFST
... JFST
... JFST!
... JFST!
... JFST!!
... JFST!!!

WAS THAT A SQUIRREL? DO SQUIRRELS MEDITATE? I WONDER... OH, MY HEAD, IT'S SO FAST.

AM I DOING THIS RIGHT? I THINK SO, I DON'T KNOW...

Post 7th Sitting Treat!

Now that you've sat 14 times, post a selfie of you with the page on the right ⟶ to social media.

#JFST   HASHTAG YOUR POST

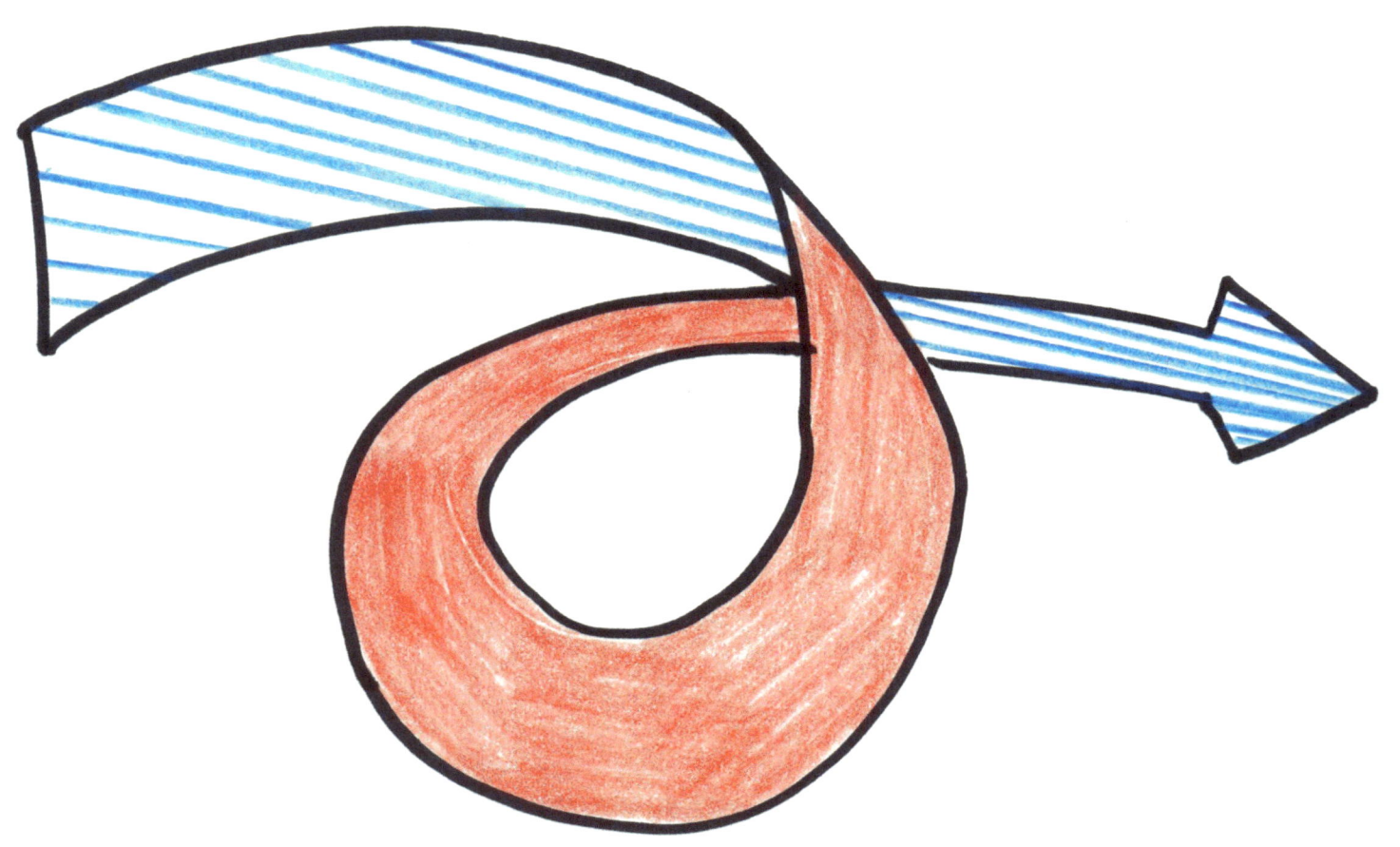

Official CERTIFICATE

of being a genuine

MEDITATOR

has been awarded to

_____

for having successfully meditated for 20 times.

_____ _____ _____
Stallion  Dragon  Rabbi Brian

Book-Club / Parent-Teen Book-Club

Download discussion questions.
Learn how to invite Rabbi Brian to join your group.
ROTB.org/meditation

#JFST

Tag your sitting on social media with #JFST
See tags: @ROTB.org/meditation

About The Authors

Rabbi Brian is an ordained rabbi who lives in Portland, Oregon with his bride, two children, and dog. His congregation – *Religion-Outside-The-Box* – can be found online at ROTB.org.

Dana & Bill Clark are a nurse and a nuclear engineer. They are creative meditators living in Pennsylvania and working on their next big artistic project – a baby!

www.ingramcontent.com/pod-product-compliance
Lightning Source LLC
Chambersburg PA
CBHW040101020526
44112CB00029B/21